What the King Likes

words by Amanda Graham
illustrated by Greg Holfeld

The king likes jumping.

The king likes climbing.

The king likes skating.

The king likes flying.

8

The king likes swinging.

The king likes riding.

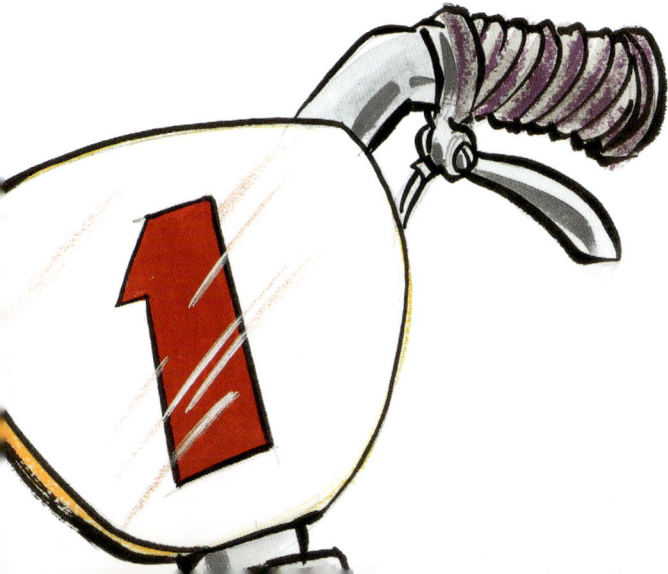

Uh oh!

The king does not
like falling.